Sermons

Sermons ©2019 by **Marream Krollos**. Published in the United States by Vegetarian Alcoholic Press. Not one part of this work may be reproduced without expressed written consent from the author. For more information, please contact vegalpress@gmail.com

Sermon for Girls 1
Moth Sermon 2
Grown Man with Freckles 3
Man, 4
Father, 5
Father, 6
Stray Pussy Cat's Sermon 7
To You for Your Mother 8
Snakes, 9
Sermon 10
Brothers and Sisters 11
Boys and Men 12
Sermon 13
The Voice Said: 14
You are the Wrong Half 15
Sermon 16
Much of your life has been about your lovers. 17
For Give and For Get 18
She likes her bed 19

He likes her 20
Sermon 21
Variations 22
It is More Natural to Forget 23
The Reflection of Sky in Patches of Water on a Desert 25
Salmon's Sermon 27
The meeting begins. 28
Reel 29
Reel 30
Spinster's Sermon 31
Packaging 32
June 33
To Happen, Next 34
It makes me romantic. 35
Read How Lonely This 36
Poets Native to Their Land Would Cut off Their Tongues to Write in Their Tongue 37
For Sake 38
Sermon for Boys 39
Sincerely, 40

Candles Without Wicks 41
Writing on Windows 42
Scientist's Sermon 43
Overpopulation 44
When You Wake Up 45
When You Grow Up 46
Christmas Sermon 47
Star of the Sea 48
Lord, 49
For Recollection 50
Parsnip's Sermon 51
War and Peace 52
Victim's Sermon 53
Sermon 54
Live 55
Cancer 56
Death Bed 57
Union Street 58
Response 59
We Called Our Star by Many Names 60

Sermon for Girls

This is what happened…

And that's why they hate us…
They do not love women anymore…
They love only other men…
With another man a man can clap onto a body like his own
and let go knowing he has done nothing wrong...
He can laugh or not laugh knowing that he is still good…
They love their brothers and their sons…
and their fathers whom they want to love them…

Somehow the things they heard women speak about them
made them so angry that they could not speak anymore…
The things they heard women speak about their brothers
hurt them so much they could not speak…

Now women make men sons
so one man can love another man…
So he can kiss his own
much smaller mouth to say
good night…

And the woman who made a man for a man can say…
I loved you so much…
I made you another man…
To love…

Moth Sermon

You cannot capture this

so you must

let this capture the cannot.

You wish to be loved for who you are

yet you must

love who you can become.

Stay in waves to move forward.

Hold on when waves retreat.

What does it take to be good?

You are not beautiful.

Make silk.

Fly faster than butterflies.

Be the one color
black and white
mean and nice
without confusion.

Grown Man with Freckles

Your face is marked
With spots
With little children

And her thighs try too
To separate
They are too much of one thing

She cannot judge the spots
Could be baby blossoms were they stranger

Your spots cannot be washed off
Her thighs cannot be cut off

Wear pretty clothes and smile
To cover you and to live in
To take off your face and thighs
The things that will not
Live only in your hands
The things you want to live in each other

Man,

This is a boring arrangement

What is on your mind
What you see right now
Your eyes embedded in your face
Your face squeezed into eyes
Messy traces of you

Traces sloughing off

You are concerned now with the sound of one of your hairs
falling to the ground
You are concerned with what you would think of her hair
falling to the ground

You were frightened when you saw her in the window
You were afraid when you saw her lying wildly with legs
apart

She scared you
when she looked at you
as if you would fit
in her mouth.

Father,

She is being mean to me again
This time she tried to fit me under the kitchen sink
She tried to tie me up and got really angry when I let her
She is beautiful like a movie star, but so cruel like an actress
I was howling at her so she would love
me but she wouldn't stare
I screamed you have to love
me too over and over and over again
You have to love the both of us I yelped
My face was open and gnawed by the
time she had finished dressing
I held on to her knees so I could kiss them no matter
how hard she beat my back

She is in love with only you
She is only in love with you

The glowered dew of her told it all

Father,

Your eyes swell shut.

Unintentionally, you
cannot see your hands
cannot find your swollen eyes.

Someday you will have a cancer.
Your cells inside
are dividing now
unintentionally
mutating into things
unlike the perfect ovals
a mother would
have wished for you to be.

Eat dying fruit and dead fish
to save yourself and protect me
from believing that the things that die
are better than the things you made.

Stray Pussy Cat's Sermon

Remember, your claws do not dull when you starve.

Your sight weakens, your muscles
your movement slows
not the sharpness of your claws.
Their strength is in sharpness
so your strength is in sharpness.

Are you lonely?
        Because you crawl

Are you hungry?
        Because you smell the meat in concrete
        Because you find the cream in leaves

Never.
What did we do wrong?
Where did we go wrong?
Ever.

To You for Your Mother

To have us
she had to harm you
a boy child
and wonder always why

we made music
as we tenderly stroked her face
we intervened only when
she refused to feed you.

In the end
she would have let you
touch her to eat
though it was too late
when she could again see others
when finally we saw her
when the sorrow seeped through her.

So now you know
you were born
weeping like your mother.

Snakes,

Why have you put your mother here?
You push her away then cling to her with your teeth.
So I can see myself clearly.
I am simple like a worm that says:

My mother
your body
was cut up
in the parts that would have given you pleasure
my body
was not cut
still I will not feel pleasure out of love for you Mother

Your life is not torture
Mother
because of what they did to you
my lack of living is proof
you don't need what I won't have
let's not feel sorry for each other.

Sermon

If we could speak
we would let you know
whom we feel pity for.

Had we not tried and failed you would never have guessed that feet sink in water. When you saw us sprawled face down on concrete, the night you tried to soar, you discovered you are not like seagulls. Had we not been willing to drink you would not have known thirst cannot be quenched in the sea. It is the cracked red skin on our faces that taught you about the dangers of living in wind. Had we not taken that first bite you would not have realized sand leaves you hungry.

If we could sing
for both of us
we would pray.

Brothers and Sisters

The people say we are not animals

because we can speak

then they forget words after the thrill of speaking diminishes

so they say we write words down

so we do not forget

then they have to leave them

all alone.

Boys and Men

I can help you with that
he barks.

I have been waiting too long
she whimpers. It would take a pack of wolves now. It
would take a pack of wolves now.

It would take
a pack of wolves
now.

 It would take a pack of wolves.

Sermon

From this age to that age the body continues growing.
Eventually, however, we begin to decay.

The God in us is born needing to be worshiped.
The bit of the almighty spirit we inherit
makes for a want to be adored.
We are, after all, our father's children.

Your desires are rabid dogs
held back by sturdy fences.
You can hear them howl.
You do not have to be afraid.

That's why
on the screen now is a woman who lost
both her boys in a war
and you won't do anything
but consider being kind if you meet her.

The Voice Said:

Woman,
Wake up and carry your heavy breasts.
Wash your face with water and dress.
Walk in the cold because the snow has come
and all people are people in the cold
when the snow comes.
Get on the bus to wonder who
has kissed whom on this bus.
And if it is not his whiskey bottle
he is holding inside his coat pocket
but his gun to shoot you in the heart
you will gladly forgive him because of all that you have
and have not done.
You will gladly have lived to finally know this
is what it feels like
to be shot in the heart.

You are the Wrong Half

You stupid slut
You are not one of those mermaids
Sailors think to swim alongside of
You are all the wrong half fish
I must remind myself

You are mostly eel
Can habitually coil
Sway and glide rolled up
Move your face towards your self
Your own thick breath feels the thin skin

Of your own
All your own

Bite with your nails scratch with your teeth
Breasts perfectly formed with deep brown irises
Teardrops with all the right half cut off
But they are only so
You can recollect yourself

Sermon

The Lord in his infinite wisdom
put these gorillas in a cage.
They hurt themselves only trying to escape.

Now they are ravenous just like the starving people.
But they will not die like the starving people
who begged for food to buy more life.

Perhaps you should starve yourself to know
what of life makes one want it.

Much of your life has been about your lovers.

All of your lovers had beautiful hair
made of liquid tissue.

Because of all they have given you
you can still chew
but only on one side of your mouth.
They taught you how to keep
in skin of different textures.
They have shown you how to sleep
to know your own size.

Though it is odd how water trickles down
the corners of their mouths
when they speak
accidentally
as they take you
as if they are made of it.

For Give and For Get

Your grandmother came to you in your sleep.
This is the woman who knew you when you still believed
you could be loved.
In the dream she was your source of strength
at a dinner party you attended naked.
You were ashamed, yet defiant. She spoke to you
as if you were not wrong.
She looked at the others as if to say she knew you
were naked, you should be naked.
You felt as if you had been mistaken. She must have always
loved you the way you were.
She must not have meant what she said about you smelling
like your father.
So, you took the opportunity to tell her who
you had become.
You told her you had found out
not all men like to slap women as she had said.

"You have never known men or life,"
she looked angry, or condescending.

You explained you had met many since she died,
patted her head, kissed her head.
But she only boasted about knowing dead men who tell all.

Her hair burned your lips.

You wondered
if she had come from heaven
if her daughter's daughter could go to heaven
if you would ever deserve to wake up.

She likes her bed

and the shapes she makes by pressing down on her eyes while her head sinks into the pillow. There is something in the back of her head, proof that evolution created her, so she forgives the mean things she said and remembers she may never be different. She may always be different because even though she cried once at the foot of their steps even though she has already committed herself to seeing them again in heaven the sense in her life is still just hoping someday they will want that about her.

He likes her

hair is dirty all over
if by knowing only
it is dirty hair

pluckable weed
that grows unchecked
taken down and
given up

unwashed hair
now that no one
will wash hair if
hair is dirty no one
will touch

hair picked and pulled
out the shredded hair
matted in the damp
forest of stench
on hair

that wants to be
kissed while not able
to respect who can
kiss hair

who can love hair
who will take hair
who would have hair
and still…

Sermon

Since he did it to you
You forget
Touch yourself all the time
The blood caked in your fingertips is your own
From last night
Before you wonder

Find reasons to put them in your mouth
Make your limbs have each other slowly
You are not your body so your body can be yours
Else you will search always for bodies

How much do you want it?
Does the wanting lift you off the bed?
Like a possessed bitch

A bitch

Variations

When she is happy hearing them speak out loud at times

makes her want to touch their mouths to her own hand waving fingers in and out of the breath of words akin to smoke rings that caress each other and let go happily satisfied

with the sweetest of sweetness coming to her from throats to mouths to hand

but when she is sad she only wants to be one of their favorite someone and she has to be naked to find something that fits right on her

so she sees then that they have nothing to say to her so she sees their sounds.

It is More Natural to Forget

Finally I left
I confess
To fall in love with you
I have traveled with a positive
Attitude and a panic

About somebody here
Look at me and say love
Call it love if I say it is love

Though you may be of a dour people
Staunch poets but strong tall people

The weather here chills my teeth
And I had hoped for weather to warm
I have walked here with this sadness
The roundness of my middle bulging
My head bursting in tender small bubbles

I came here for you and you saw something
You do not want as I hoped you would
So I write now though I had hoped
I would have no time for these
Questions from a time before travel

Even with those dry hands and rough faces
All of you
You are all your own celebrated fair-haired maidens

But I still want to ask you about the sun
What it feels like when you don't see it
And tell you about the first time I saw snow

Because this is fear
On me if you will not
Help me contain it
It will have us both

Your land is green but I am not impressed
It is not white
I prefer blue

I like royal blue on hills and fields
I like sapphire grass and sapphire weeds

It is unoriginal
I know
To want earth to silently meet the sea
Still
I am unimpressed by your green land

Grass so rich you say it drips
As I go stale here seeping of something

You think it is beautiful here
Though everywhere the stars
Cannot make wishes

Though everywhere there are corners
Begging to hide

Because this is too heavy to drop
Here too this hovers out of sight

Here too I wonder why even a light
Can be half the light it used to be

The Reflection of Sky in Patches of Water on a Desert

It is all so obvious now
All right in front of you

Water was once together
Then it separated
Into separate strands
Of its separate selves

Sun is scarce here
It puts pressure on your skin
Clamps down on your skin
Cold found under your skin

As knees bend and ache
Knees more than just bone
Knees have brought you

To this glacier
This a white desert
You have come with knees
To see desert
To see how desert
Is beautiful still

To know some ice
Cannot contain molten rock
That becomes the land
A mind slowly curdling out
Imagining it wants to be
Trampled on
Covered by moss

Blue sky in this clear water
On a black desert of cooled lava
That had bubbled and raged red once
While the people stayed cold blooded
No lava under their skin

That boils with want

This mountain of clay
Shaped by hands
Squeezed and molded
Glazed with green
The people speak of sulfur
The people speak of age
The earth's crust writhes

This mountain is silent
She stays still wondering
Why do I swelter and swell
If I only spilled
If I only am
Unintentionally

You try to reach like the glacier
It too has perspired over time
Attempting the climb
Over the mountain
To reach its people

But the land here is skin
Like you it is skin
It parts to be filled
Risking all dark scars
Risking its own uniqueness
Unoriginal to its people
The land is made and remade
Only heat from under the sea
Like all land is

Salmon's Sermon

To be free is to be wild
they say
to search to spawn to seek
is wild.

Now even you, pink fleshed fish
do not live in the sea.

You and your young
farmed in foreign water.

You must feel
the heart in this piece.

This piece
is a scarecrow
You want it to have a heart.

You must understand
even now you are wild.

The meeting begins.

All the men say this air is not good. We need good air

or we will stop breathing.

A girl stands up while crushing

small blue and green flowers in her hands.

The girl says I know I want to live.

I know my lungs are better

than my bones because they rise and fall on their own.

I know my lungs are better than my heart…

All the men stand up and say no, Sweetheart, your heart

does too, so does your heart. Your heart rises

and falls on its own too, Sweetheart.

But my heart needs blood to make it …

No, Sweetheart, so do your lungs.

They need the blood from your heart.

Well now you've done it.

You've ruined everything for me. This is impossible

like asking a man to make another man love you.

Now I have nothing.

Now go and tell other girls about air.

Reel

You cut this bread for yourself
You fall asleep by yourself

You dream of women without faces

Who is who?
We are all a knife

Whose stairs are these?

Then falls everything
You seeing you every time
Only you are alive always

This key this
Key to everywhere
Also a knife

You fall
Even these stairs won't have you

This bread
This bed
A grave for yourself

Reel

One river flows up from your feet
From your head another flows down

They meet in your salty middle
To form a salty swell

What if every cell explodes out of every pore?
It would leave you to soak in your own sea

Touch this please

Your soul swell
It starts in your chest
But must crawl down
To where your self wants

Exit

If you stuff me, Sir
If you fill me up, Mister

Barricade the portals
Block the openings
That can serve as doors

You would only keep me from spilling

Spinster's Sermon

A woman once lived here alone. She was very quiet. She watched television often and occasionally enjoyed a cup of coffee with her cigarettes. Then, she died and began to rot. Her heart stopped, her body decayed right where she sat. Her favorite show was on television at the time, and there was a cup of coffee beside her.

None of us knew she had died until we smelled something. We broke down her door and went inside. We were all curious, so we cut her chest open to look at her heart. Would it be fleshy or dry, red or blue? We found she had no more blood to give us; it had all congealed in her veins. Her heart was dry, small, and brown. We removed it and put it away for safe keeping in a small wooden box.

Maybe she was kind, maybe she was not. We do not know if she was kind or not. But she must not have been touched or talked to for a long time. She must have known it would end this way. Had she not realized, her heart may have still been pink with anticipation.

Perhaps she sought company every time someone passed by her door. Perhaps her then wet heart skipped a beat when she thought she would receive it. We do not know. We will keep her heart here in this small wooden box to remind us of how lucky we all are.

Packaging

Organs are so funny
Their tissue is so fragile
This funny type of weak

All it takes is one good puncture
One terrible tear or right rip
Specific appropriate cut
And the living in them moves out

So you take this spoon to your gut, Samurai

Pick it up
Hold it tight
No!
With both hands
That's right
Stretch your arms out
Quickly drive it in

That's it
Good girl!
That's how skin breaks
That's how blood leaks

That's how you become a samurai
The warrior you have always wanted

June

This is June

The sun comes
A moment in
Which do you remember?
When somebody said you have a scar over your right eye
You did not believe them
Why didn't you?
Really do I?
Really do I? With a smile

This is June here
It looks like this

The windows are open
Behind the woman who is behind a bar
There is no danger of cold
The cold is gone

But it comes back

Do you want to remember?
When men used to say things
"I would marry her if she would have me."
When men used to feel that
When you saw a man smoking so hard
He was using his face to eat smoke
Nobody now likes smoke
The men don't smoke like that anymore
The men don't want to marry or smoke
The men say things like,
"You have nice tits."

To her behind the bar
Even though you are sitting there
Even while it is warm and the window is open

To Happen, Next

One minute you are trying
In the neck
Like a corner, I know

I am the little, you say
Antagonize is what I did
To destroy your relationship
With your, as long as
You don't really mean it

Because girls are just so
And boys, honestly you are going
To have to act on it

Their sleep methods get closer
And closer, you should
Scream or
Just wash away

It makes me romantic.

It is so romantic.
How you carry with you a pouch of blood.
If I look at you long enough I can almost see it.

(A jellyfish sac
filled with baby blood
full
empty
smells
fills
empty
flesh food in a jelly bag)

It hurts you.

It makes me romantic.
I put my hands there where it must be.
I imagine little drops of blood trying to defy gravity.

(Trying to be rich
thicker
resisting
wanting not to fall
red
dripping slowly
dying slowly
while trying not)

Hurting you.

Read How Lonely This

Read how lonely this is
We are not the same
Not enough the same to live in this
The one house
We are not the same
Not enough the same as all the others to leave it

But no one else has seen me naked so many times
(with legs open)
(with legs closed)
(with legs crossed)
Sitting standing or lying down naked
As you have or as I have heard
You tell me those stories about your father
(your father angry)
(your father singing)
(your father gone)

You do not like me to explain why I hurt you
Nor do I like you to explain why you hurt me
In that we are the same

And you are more the same to me than all the others
And still we are not the same enough for this one house

Poets Native To Their Land Would Cut Off Their Tongues To Write In Their Tongue

A poet
native to this land
asked to write
in my tongue

Asked to cut off my tongue
so he can write poems

Poems about the sadness
that came when I
the conqueror did not rush
to embrace him

When I set foot on his shores
and did not rush to him

Poems about how much a poet could have believed
in souls if I had rushed to hold him

For Sake

Thank you for turning away from my breasts.

I'm so welcomed for the turning of your head.

All bared I am more like my bile.

You are gallant if nothing else speaks.

This is how slight you want so much.

This is how much a mature man

you are.

Sermon for Boys

There was a boy...
He had a girl...
He was like a girl...
He cried...
His body...
They were the same...
They were different...
They were happy...
Even though they had different bodies...

Then the bad men came to hurt her...
She could not fight them because her body was small...
He could not fight them because there were so many...
They both became sad...

He stopped speaking to her...
They stopped speaking to each other...
They kept everything in their different bodies...

Sometimes she would reach out and try to touch his face...
As if he were her own girl...
Or boy she made from her body...
This only made things worse...

He would think...
I am a man
and you are a woman...

Sincerely,

You three beaks
have come to tweet of
this day's lies.

Remind us of
what is severed
when we entreat.

You three beaks
without hearts to bleed or
sleeves on which to place
a heart.

Three birds
now cannot
drink or sing or eat.

Candles Without Wicks

You cannot die.

You are not melted achingly slow.
You are not molded by the weight of a flame.
There is no heat to eat at you from the inside out.
There is no torch yanking at your heart.
Fire does not tuck at your middle.
Fire does not light up your core.

You do not know your center.

You do not know.

Writing on Windows

If you move
These letters around enough
You will begin to see them in different places
They will become different things

If you move letters around enough
You die for a while and see

        Yellow bodies
        splitting
        gelled light.

Now you know who God is
You can judge
Whether you want God
Whether God is good
For you whether sitting
With only letters to give
You are any good to God

Scientist's Sermon

Nature is the deceiver
It fools and deludes
It makes you act on illusions:

A mother's sacrifice
a man's love
a friend's need.

Liquids pumped all through you
Fluids that say bond and mate
Substances in your brain make you hate

Hormones just made you stop and smell some flowers

Overpopulation

The heartrending secret lives of seals
The black things that live in water

Where it is cold and dark they breathe
Where it is bleak and stark they breed

They crowd together out of necessity
They huddle in groups for shelter

Their limbs are joined nightly for safety
Their coupling is ignorance and bliss

When You Wake Up

I had a dream about being shot
A man put a gun against my body
He screamed, ranted, and pulled the trigger
It was not the pain like that of a cut
It was more like the pain of pressure
Lead that took and moved over my organs
I tasted the steel iron of blood rushing up my throat
When I knew I had died I woke up

I had a dream about my brother disappearing
I felt disbelief and regret
I fell to the ground sobbing
I squealed and squirmed
Yelled his name out loud to bring him back
Threw my arms up in the air to catch him
Remembered all the times I could have been better
When I knew he had died I woke up

I had a dream about floating cakes
Rich moist soft creamy cakes
They were decorated with candy
They smelled like sugar baking
I tried to grab bits and pieces
They flew too fast and too far away
Just as one came towards me

You woke up

When You Grow Up

They are so pretty you will want to have one
to wear like a ring
Make it yours

Then you are too busy pecking at crumbs for them to flee
These little hummingbirds about to be crushed

Though it is good when they die
One by one
Drop to your floor limp
Like bats or rats

It is so good
Once you understand
Good
When you realize
Once you know

Some things
just can't be done
my son.

Christmas Sermon

Abraham begot Isaac
Isaac begot and his sons begot others
Until Christ was begot

And of course David was begot
After of course Solomon was then begot by David
Christ was begot

Jacob begot Joseph the husband of Mary
Mary begot Christ

Who begot Mary?
Eve and Ruth and Jezebel

Christ was begot by men
Though only Mary and the Spirit
Gave him his body

Then Christ begot the staunchness of Peter
Christ begot the harshness of Paul
Christ begot the torment of Judas
Christ has begot

Christ was begot
Now the birth of Jesus was as follows:

Star of the Sea

You did not know what color your milk would be.

You slept after the light vanished after it spoke.

You could not die because God would live.

You felt something move inside you.

You knew God leaves a body after he has been put there by God.
You thought God comes from woman as man comes from God.

You knew you would look like God.

You want to know if God hurts in a belly.

You are where God lived.

You want to know if God hurt your belly.

The mother of God the father.

Lord,

That tingling stream
has eroded and split you
into a canyon.
Nothing fills you now
that you are bottomless.

Even before he let you know
his body shifted slowly off of yours.
You knew you would be

something that chews and spits.

You say you deserve better
but you only crave more to feed
indignity before it escapes.

You understand

It is not that you do not know why
you should not want him.
It is that you know too well why
he should not want you.

For Recollection

You cannot make everything without a
sadness.

The water in rain does not come some of the time.
By the time it had the thirst was so strong

your flesh had drunk a lot of your blood.

These thoughts do not want to purge you to day.
Something larger inside you must have already
rotted.

We know at times it is not worth all this.
How what ignores us reminds us of God.

Parsnip's Sermon

I am always mistaken about how to be kind
About how short the path to worship can be
I am a suspended thought in the mind of a liar
I would be lost in the sky were the earth not so spacious
Knowing myself has made me scared for the good

But if you froze in this dirt with me
We would drink the ground, repeat until tired but still scared
We wouldn't have to forgive the times we judged
Or wonder why all the music only made us more jagged

We both agree the voice of man makes things live
We desire someone whose many strands make him plain
Someone who eats what we are worth and says nothing
We will love his mouth and hands and wait for spring

You could give me words and I could give to you
Reason to keep buried
The brown around us mild compared to our spirits

War and Peace

Some men will love a woman so hard
They will wait and wait for her for so long
They want to kiss her and hold her again and again
This is tender of them and tenderness is good

For this reason alone the other men must pound on our flesh
For this reason only they gather their fists round our meat

For flesh that is meat that is murder

Just so one of us knows she has herself a good man

Victim's Sermon

You have not had to survive a massacre
You are jealous of those who can sleep
You thank God for your health
Though you want something of his creation
To be a type of carnation
The drama of having a womb
The romance to hold a gaze

You want to be able to make music

You want to slap your own face
You want to shred your hair to make music
Scratch at your feet to hear music
You want to pick at the skin of your face
You want to saw at your teeth until you are
The music a man can make

You do not because you should not you will not

You are normal
You are more normal than this
You are more normal than you are

Sermon

You are a natural. You can eat this poison
like a fish, like a bird, and write
hoping that it means something.
You are lovely.

And there is a reason for those who have died
and why they are too angry to tell you
what heaven is like or how to keep
out of hell.

The dead are brave.
They know fear of death
is not what keeps you alive.
They know wanting bread
did not feed them.

Live

You imagine one can be good
Wonder what more can be taken
    from the lips
The pebble you are   the center
    wants to hermit
Follow it   think of the north
        where the air sprays from your pores
        where you may be flawless

With your mind   take your body

Touch your hands intentionally
Cry more easily
Leave sex   your sixth sense
    in God's hands

This will keep your eyes breathing
Twirling over signs and tombstones
Reading reasons

Cancer

It is hard to know
How to kindly divide
But we divide anyway
Improperly sometimes
We know not what we do sometimes
We split deformed and imperfect
Are born ugly one after the other
So need to huddle together
Console each other
We the cells of you
Ate too much
Got angry
Smelled bad
Locating each other and comforting
Saying the wrong things again
Doing these bad things always
We grow in numbers and don't realize
We too will die because of this
We are only happy finally to think we are
The safety in numbers

Death Bed

Listen, I'm sorry you sometimes said funny things and
nobody laughed; remember the times you were serious and
everyone thought it was funny.
but it bothered me so much

besides
everybody except me
wants to live by the sea
Well, we are made mostly of water.

and they so often write of a desire to fly
Yes, I agree we have no empathy for the weight of wings.
We do not understand how sky thrashes.
We don't know the hell of having to keep flying for lack of
somewhere to land.
We have no sympathy for eagles, hawks, or vultures.
We don't consider that at times one would have to keep
flying for fear of having
to land.

Union Street

I know
I know
I know
When you wake up still
Knowing somebody who said they love you
Who you do not know anymore
It is not like a nightmare as much as the feeling of a face
pressed against glass
Always watching birds be birds
We know
We know
We know
Everything should come in three
First there is a man
Then a woman
Then a child
They all chant
This is what matters
But if you still want to believe in the multitudes
You may think of grains making sand only one thing
You may think of leaves playing together once pressed
against wind making the sound of all the black
And white witches
Of the world
Whispering in unison

Response

His body leaning against the doorway, he had limped to stare at the sun. The sun was so large and so hot, it was so big that day that when that thin layer of wispy white cloud came and hid him, it changed everything he understood about life.

He now understood everything. He understood now how mind could cover matter, his mind, could take over matter. He looked up and prayed, finally. God, what did you feel when they cut off my foot? What do you see, God? Why did you make us, little birds who only sing when they are too hungry, or too full? Dogs who wait to watch the sunrise? He went inside and wrote a letter. In reference to your reference to poverty being like a ship... I have to say... I disagree completely... I regret to tell you...

This explained everything. He now understood everything.

How else are people supposed to speak? They have to learn to speak. Yes, the whole body is a mouth. We bend to hide teeth and tongue. That is why all people learn to dance by kissing. And also why they have to learn to eat. So, they can learn to speak. But, what does he do when he wants to shut, he wondered.

He had moved away from the sun.

We Called Our Star by Many Names

First a stone struck a head
Then the stone was sharpened to make a blade
a knife
a sword
a rifle
a gun
shrapnel
a bomb
an atomic bomb
a hydrogen bomb
Now we know the wine by the radiation in the earth of the grape
There will be no more apes
no more fish
no more bees
the giraffes
the tigers
Muck and dirt and shit and blood were all that was
on the streets of the cities once
intestines and waste
horses
people
in the rivers
in the air
metal and glass
plastic
styrofoam
hard bags of
a ton of flesh and cake and fruit in the bags
The people could not stop
Too tired they needed to put something in a bottle
to give gifts made of sharp and dull
Sad and lonely they needed a small thing to place
or look at that day
to make them believe some day...
They were all alone
They were never alone

They positioned themselves to pout in pain
They put liquids in pottery to honor people
who would have had them
traveling thirsty they could not just drink out of their hands
rape within the tribe
rape of other tribes
rape of distant tribes
rape of lands and cultures
Something everybody has done cannot be wrong
The smoke eventually disappeared

but when I look at your face
I know we will not die
The weapons will not reach us
Our bodies will take in each blast
keep it let it live in our tissue
make us electric
We will eat when we find something soft
to put in our mouths
Some things are not pure radiation
in a room with metal bars on windows to live
out the weather
We will be rare like black bears and white birds
We will live the last of our kind
because when I look at your face
when I touch it with my hands
I wish I were blind so I could only know
your face with hands
There are words still
and laughing thoughts
I am and you are
We roll into each other and pleasure
still makes you stronger and me weaker
It is not water
It is not air
It is your voice
when the shards cut your throat
It is your skin
When that melts
it is your bones

www.ingramcontent.com/pod-product-compliance
Lightning Source LLC
Chambersburg PA
CBHW060506080526
44584CB00015B/1566